Brisbane Secrets.  *Go and What to Do for a Memorable Trip*

CRAVEDM CREATIONS

Copyright © 2023 CravedM Creations

All rights reserved.

All rights reserved. No part of this book may be reproduced, stored in a retrieval system, or transmitted in any form or by any means, electronic, mechanical, photocopying, recording, or otherwise, without the prior written permission of the publisher, except for brief quotations in critical reviews or articles.

Published by CravedM Creations

Cover Design by CravedM Creations

Visit our website at
https://thewordmoment.wordpress.com/blog/

For inquiries, please contact
wiseravenbrisbane@gmail.com

Distributed by Amazon

DEDICATION

To the spirited explorers and wanderers seeking the hidden gems of Brisbane, may this guide be your compass to uncovering the city's best-kept secrets.

Embrace the essence of Brisbane, create lasting memories, and let each moment become a chapter in your memorable journey.

Here's to discovering the soul of the city and creating a tapestry of memories that linger long after your journey ends.

Happy travels, and may Brisbane's secrets reveal themselves to you in all their splendour!

CONTENTS

Initiation to Brissie Vibe — 12
- From the Airport to the City's Heart — 13
- Must-Dos for Different Arrivals — 18

A Thrifty Guide to Blending In: Weaving into Brisbane's Fabric — 20
- Exploring the Local Markets — 20
- Things you will see at a typical Brisbane Market — 22
- Tips for Thrifty Explorers: — 23
- Choosing Local Over Convenience — 25

Footsteps and Echoes of Time: Take a walk in Brisbane City Centre like a local. — 27
- Walking in the Tracks of History: A Path of Discovery — 27

Spiritual Oasis Amidst Urban Splendour: Exploring Historical Places of Worship in Brisbane — 29

Climate and Seasons — 31

South Bank: A Cultural Tapestry Unveiled — 34
- South Bank Parklands: Nature's Oasis in the Urban Canvas — 34
- Wheel of Brisbane: A Spiralling Panorama Above the River's Serenade — 35
- My favourites: Additional South Bank Gems — 36

Fortitude Valley (the Valley): Where the Night Comes Alive — 37
- Nightlife Extravaganza: Bars, Clubs, and Live Music Venues — 38
- Daytime Exploration: James Street Precinct — 38
- Valley Vignettes: Exploring the Eclectic — 39
- Brisbane's Chinatown: A Culinary Odyssey — 39

New Farm: A Tranquil Haven of Greenery and Gastronomy — 40

Indooroopilly Island Conservation Park: A Tranquil Retreat in Nature's Embrace ... 42

Explore the Brisbane River: A CityCat Symphony ... 43

University of Queensland: Academic Oasis and Blooms of Spring ... 46

Eat Street Northshore: A Culinary Carnival Under the Stars ... 49

- Foodie Wonderland: A Treasure Trove of Culinary Delights ... 50
- Asian Street Food Extravaganza: Flavours from Every Corner ... 50
- Gourmet Dessert Oasis: Sweet Temptations ... 51
- Lively Atmosphere ... 51

Mt. Coot-tha: A Summit Serenade of Panoramic Splendour 52

- Hiking Elevation: A Nature-Infused Ascent ... 52
- Scenic Drive: Effortless Elevation to Magnificent Views ... 52

Brisbane Botanic Gardens: Tranquility at the Mountain's Feet ... 53

- Leisurely Stroll: Botanical Bliss in Every Step ... 54

Moreton Island: An Aquatic Wonderland of Adventure and Serenity ... 55

- Ferry Ride: A Seafaring Prelude to Paradise ... 56
- Snorkelling Extravaganza: Underwater Marvels Unveiled ... 56
- Sandboarding Thrills: Dunes of Endless Adventure ... 57
- Dolphin Feeding: Sunset Serenade with Marine Companions ... 57
- Relaxation Haven: Balmy Beaches and Tranquil Retreats ... 58

Bribie Island: Coastal Serenity Unveiled ... 59

- Sun-Drenched Haven 59
- Exploring Nature's Sanctuary 59
- Aquatic Exploration 59
- Breathtaking Sunset Spectacle 59
- Stradbroke Island: Coastal Paradise Unveiled 60
  - Island Gateway: Crossing the Waters 61
  - Sandy Shores and Turquoise Waters: Island Bliss 61
  - Exploring the Diverse Landscapes: Nature's Tapestry 61
  - Marine Adventures: Aquatic Wonderland 61
  - Sunset Serenade: Nature's Farewell 62
- Lone Pine Koala Sanctuary: An Aussie Wildlife Haven 62
- Embrace the Outdoors: Brisbane's Active Lifestyle 64
  - Café Culture: Sip and Savour in Brisbane's Charm 65
  - Learn the Lingo: Aussie Slang 101 65
  - Cheer for the Local Teams: Brisbane's Sporting Spirit 66
- Brisbane Festival: A September Extravaganza 68
  - The Ekka: August Extravaganza 68
  - Brisbane Asia Pacific Film Festival: Cinematic Celebration .. 69

Acknowledgements

I would like to express my deepest gratitude and heartfelt appreciation to God, the source of all wisdom and inspiration. Without His guidance and grace, this book would not have been possible. I am humbled and in awe of His unending love and support throughout the writing process.

I want to acknowledge His divine hand in every word written, every idea conceived, and every twist and turn of the story. His wisdom and direction have been my compass, leading me through the creative journey with unwavering assurance.

With heartfelt gratitude to the vibrant city of Brisbane and its welcoming community. Your secrets have been our treasures, and this guide is a testament to the shared joy of exploration. Cheers to the memories made and those yet to be uncovered!

Chapter 1: Unveiling Brisbane's Soul

G'day, and Embrace the Brisbanite Way

Welcome to the vibrant tapestry of Brisbane, a place that transcends the boundaries of a mere city—it's an embodiment of a lifestyle. But let me assure you, this travel guide is not your typical tourist manual. Over my five-year love affair with Brisbane, I've gathered stories and experiences that I'm thrilled to share with you. This guide is a window into the heart of the city, allowing you to blend in, worship, and savour your visit with insider tales that will transform your journey into a true Brisbanite experience.

Brisbane: A City, A Lifestyle

Brisbane isn't just a destination; it's a canvas upon which life's vivid moments are painted. The laughter of locals blending harmoniously with the river's gentle murmur tells tales of a city that dances to its own rhythm. Through my stories, you'll uncover the pulse of Brisbane, its hidden corners, and the essence of a lifestyle that embraces the simple joys of existence.

A Thrifty Guide to Blending In

This guide isn't about ticking off a checklist of sights; it's about becoming a part of the city's fabric. You'll journey through local markets, hearing the traders' stories as they peddle their wares. You'll hop onto buses with stories to share, and your footsteps will resonate with the stories of those who've walked before. By weaving in my personal encounters, you'll discover how to stretch your budget while immersing yourself in Brisbane's vibrant life.

Spiritual Oasis Amidst Urban Splendour

Beyond the iconic landmarks lie places of worship that hold not just architectural beauty but also the stories of those who gather within. These stories become woven into the very fabric of your visit as you experience Brisbane's spiritual tapestry firsthand. You'll discover how places of worship aren't just structures but gateways to understanding the city's rich cultural tapestry.

Weathering the Cultural Landscape

As you dive into Brisbane's lifestyle, I'll sprinkle in personal anecdotes that will make your experiences truly insider affairs. Through my stories, you'll come to appreciate the art of fitting in—whether it's relishing a morning coffee at a café with a tale of its own or standing shoulder-to-shoulder with locals, cheering during a sports match. These stories will transform you from a mere observer to a cherished participant in Brisbane's cultural landscape.

Your Brisbane Odyssey Begins

This isn't just a travel guide; it's an invitation to join me on a journey through the soul of Brisbane. As you embark on this adventure, keep in mind that this guide is not bound by conventional norms. It's an invitation to step into the shoes of a Brisbanite, to savour the stories etched into its streets, and to create your own stories that will intertwine with those of the city. Brisbane isn't just a place you visit; it's a place you experience, and with this guide, you'll embark on a journey that's as unique and vivid as the city itself.

Initiation to Brissie Vibe

Brisbane thrives on a unique blend of sun-soaked days and friendly locals who seem to have mastered the art of being perpetually relaxed. As you step off the plane and into the heart of Queensland's capital, you'll immediately sense the laid-back charm that defines the city. Even from the airport, you'll be greeted by warm smiles and the famous Australian hospitality that sets the tone for your visit.

Photo by Josh Withers on Unsplash-Available for hire

From the Airport to the City's Heart

Photo by Tobby Scott on Arkhefield.com

Brisbane Airport isn't just a gateway; it's a glimpse into the city's welcoming spirit. The staff's genuine friendliness is your first taste of the Brissie vibe. If hunger strikes, the airport's array of restaurants—ranging from local favourites to international cuisines—will ensure your taste buds are satisfied. And don't forget to explore the duty-free shops for a chance to pick up unique Australian products and souvenirs before you even step foot in the city.

Australia offers a delightful array of unique products and souvenirs that make for perfect keepsakes from your journey.

Here's a list of distinctive Australian items I took notice of when I first arrived in Brisbane, and you can pick them up from Brisbane Airport (BNE) to spruce up your Brisbanite experience:

1. Go Card: Get a Go Card immediately after you step off the plane. Go Card is a cheaper means to travel around the city on all Translink buses, trains (including Airtrain), ferry, and tram services in greater Brisbane, Ipswich, Moreton Bay, Redlands, Sunshine Coast, and Gold Coast regions.
2. Tim Tams: These iconic chocolate biscuits are a beloved Australian treat. Grab a few packs in various flavours to savour back home.
3. Kangaroo Leather Products: Look for wallets, belts, and bags made from kangaroo leather—a durable and uniquely Australian material.

   I didn't know kangaroo leather was a thing, but later in my stay in Brisbane, I learned that it is a thing!
4. Akubra Hat: Embrace the outback spirit with a traditional Akubra hat, a staple of rural Australian culture.

   These are very high priced at the airport. I will suggest buying them only if you are a hat person.
5. Ugg Boots: Keep your feet cosy with genuine Australian sheepskin Ugg boots, perfect for chilly nights.

   I know there have been some controversies about the origin of the Ugg boots in the past with the US-based Deckers Outdoor Corporation and the torture the Merino sheep are placed through just to produce the shoes, but they are really an Australian thing.
6. Macadamia Nuts: Taste the buttery goodness of macadamia nuts, a native Australian treat available in various flavours.

During my early days in Brisbane, I struggled to know what the fuss about the Macadamia nuts was, but I learned that they are actually indigenous to southeastern Queensland and have a lot of health and nutritional benefits. Macadamia nuts are rich in vitamins, minerals, fibre, and antioxidants. When substituted for snacks, they can help with weight loss, improved gut health, and protection against conditions like diabetes or heart disease.

Disclaimer: I don't have any health professional backing here. These are things the locals told me when I asked.

Suggestion: When I tried the nuts in 2015, I tried the coffee and vanilla-flavoured ones, and it was good.

7. Australian Wines: Pick up a bottle of Australian wine featuring world-renowned labels from the country's finest vineyards.

    Suggestion: I am not that much of an alcohol person, so I wouldn't have much to say here. The only world-renowned Australian-based wine I have tried is the Yellow Tail wine. I tried it at a team night-out event in 2017. A colleague suggested it because of its unique fruit-forward wines.

    Disclaimer: The company has not paid me to say this. This is a personal opinion based on what I have tried.

8. Australian Wildlife Plush Toys: Choose from a variety of stuffed animals representing Australia's unique wildlife, from koalas to kangaroos.

9. Boomerangs: Whether for display or as a fun

activity, a boomerang makes for a unique Australian souvenir.
10. Australian Skincare Products: Pamper yourself with skincare products infused with native Australian ingredients like tea tree oil, eucalyptus, and Kakadu plum.
With the skincare products, I have many suggestions, but I will not make any suggestions for now because it will take up space. I will leave it to you to try the different tea tree oils and eucalyptus oils Australia has to offer for yourself.

Remember, these souvenirs aren't just items; they're memories you can hold in your hands. Each product carries a piece of Australia's culture, heritage, and natural beauty, making your Brisbanite journey even more unforgettable.

Image by Sunshine Coast News

BRISBANE UNVEILED

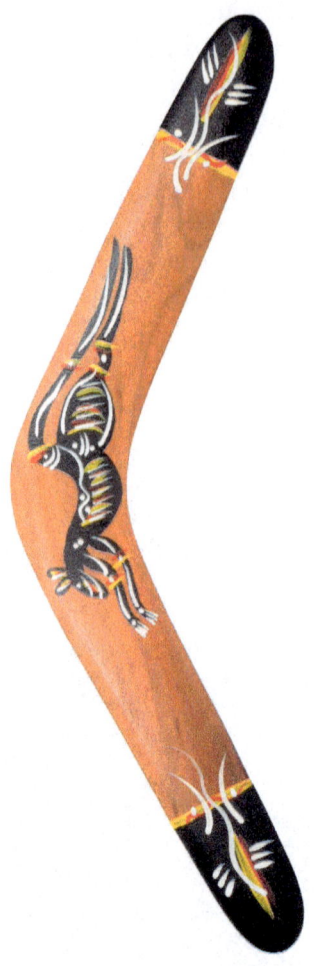

Image by kstudio on Freepik

Must-Dos for Different Arrivals

Arriving in the Morning

If you're a morning traveller, start your day with a riverside stroll along the iconic Brisbane River. Head to the Kangaroo Point Cliffs to catch panoramic views of the city as the morning sun paints the sky. Afterwards, head to a local café for your first Aussie brekkie—an experience you won't want to miss.

- → Kangaroo Point is free to enter
- → Kangaroo Point is easily accessible by foot, bicycle, or car. The area is open to the public and offers various vantage points to enjoy the scenery.
- → Kangaroo Point features a range of public art installations, including sculptures and murals, adding an artistic touch to the natural environment.
- → Kangaroo Point is positioned directly across from Brisbane's central business district. The cliffs offer panoramic views of the city skyline, Brisbane River, and the iconic Story Bridge.

Arriving in the Afternoon

For those landing in the afternoon, make your way to South Bank Parklands. Unwind at Streets Beach, a man-made lagoon with golden sands, or explore the park's walking trails. As the sun begins to set, find a vantage point along the river to witness the stunning skyline come alive with lights.

- → South Bank Parklands is free to enter
- → South Bank Parklands has free WiFi access
- → The Wheel of Brisbane, a giant Ferris wheel located in South Bank, offers breathtaking aerial

- → South Bank boasts the popular Streets Beach—a man-made beach with a sparkling lagoon, providing locals and visitors a unique opportunity to enjoy a beach experience in the heart of the city.
- → The parklands are home to over 5,000 subtropical plant species, creating a lush environment that supports local biodiversity.
- → South Bank is home to various cultural institutions, including the Queensland Art Gallery, Gallery of Modern Art (GOMA), and the Queensland Museum, offering a diverse range of exhibitions and experiences.
- → Within the parklands, you'll find the Epicurious Garden—a dedicated space where visitors can explore and learn about edible plants while enjoying a tranquil setting.
- → A well-maintained riverfront promenade offers a picturesque pathway for walkers, joggers, and cyclists to enjoy the scenic Brisbane River.
- → The South Bank Boat Pool provides a safe environment for novice rowers and kayakers to practice their skills, offering a unique aquatic experience within the city.
- → The South Bank area is dotted with restaurants, cafes, and eateries that serve up a range of cuisines, allowing visitors to savour local and international flavours.
- → South Bank features a collection of public art sculptures and installations, adding an artistic touch to the urban landscape.

views of the city and parklands, making it a popular attraction.

Arriving in the Evening

If you arrive in the evening, treat yourself to a leisurely dinner at one of Brisbane's riverside restaurants. The Story Bridge comes alive with colourful lights, creating a mesmerising backdrop for your meal. Afterwards, take a stroll along the river, where you'll feel the city's energy as you immerse yourself in the vibrant night scene.

A Thrifty Guide to Blending In: Weaving into Brisbane's Fabric

Exploring the Local Markets

Venture beyond the tourist traps and step into the world of Brisbane's local markets. As you stroll through stalls adorned with handmade crafts, fresh produce, and unique treasures, you'll be more than a passerby. Feel the warmth of community connections as you engage in conversations that go beyond transactions, capturing a slice of Brisbane's authenticity.

Imagine Brisbane's local markets as a bustling bazaar where stories are bartered, memories are sold, and the currency exchanged is not just dollars but a shared passion for life. Picture yourself weaving through stalls that resemble kaleidoscopes of culture and creativity. Each stall is a tapestry that artisans and traders have woven, carrying with them a piece of their history, their aspirations, and their creativity. As you meander through this marketplace of dreams, you're not just a spectator—you're a participant, joining a symphony of voices that sing the melody of humanity.

Here are some popular local markets in Brisbane that I frequented when I was there:

→ South Bank Lifestyle Markets: These markets at South Bank Parklands offer a range of handmade arts and crafts, clothing, accessories, and unique souvenirs. Open on weekends. They provide a picturesque riverside setting.

→ Brisbane City Markets: Held in Reddacliff Place in the heart of the city, these markets feature local artisans and designers showcasing their handmade creations.

→ Eagle Farm Markets: This market offers fresh produce, gourmet foods, baked goods, and unique handmade crafts. It's a great place to enjoy a leisurely Sunday morning.

→ Kelvin Grove Village Markets: Located near the QUT Kelvin Grove campus, these markets provide a mix of fresh produce, handmade goods, clothing, and vintage finds.

→ Davies Park Market: Situated in the West End, this market is known for its community atmosphere and diverse offerings, including fresh produce, arts and crafts, clothing, and food stalls.

→ Boundary Street Markets: Another gem in the West End, these markets feature a range of international street food stalls, vintage clothing, arts, and live music.

→ West End Farmers Market: A popular Saturday morning hot spot, you can rely on the West End Markets for your dose of locally grown fresh produce, live local music, and breezy riverside views.

NB: All these places are easily accessible by public transport. Visit queensland.com/au/en/places-to-see/ to get a complete list of markets in Brisbane

Photo by Andy Wang on Unsplash-Available for hire

Things you will see at a typical Brisbane Market

In this vibrant bazaar, your senses will be intoxicated by the array of handmade crafts, fresh produce, and unique treasures from across the globe. Here, artisans craft jewellery that tells tales of distant lands, potters shape clay into vessels that hold the whispers of artisans' hands, and painters capture the essence of nature on canvases that breathe life. The aroma of fresh produce mingles with the scent of spices, taking you on a culinary journey.

This is a realm where you'll uncover treasures like

→ Handmade Crafts: Intricately carved wooden sculptures, hand-painted ceramics, woven textiles that bear the stories of generations, and jewellery that carries the magic of distant lands.
→ Fresh Produce: A cornucopia of colours and flavours—juicy tropical fruits, farm-fresh vegetables, and exotic herbs that infuse the air with their fragrance.
→ Unique Treasures: Antique trinkets, vintage books that carry the whispers of readers past, and one-of-a-kind curiosities that hold secrets and stories.
→ Street Food from All Cultures: A World on a Plate

As your senses dance through the bazaar, your taste buds will be equally delighted by street food from every corner of the world. Embrace the diversity of flavours as you savour dishes that tell tales of family recipes, culinary traditions, and the fusion of cultures. Whether you're enjoying fragrant curries, crispy empanadas, mouthwatering dumplings, or sweet treats that melt in your mouth, each bite is a passport to a different world.

Tips for Thrifty Explorers:

→ Bring Your Own Shopping Bag: To reduce waste and embrace eco-friendliness, carry your reusable shopping bag to carry your newfound treasures.
→ Cash is King: While many stalls accept card payments, having cash on hand will make your transactions smoother, especially with smaller vendors.
→ Watch Out for Our Furry Friends: Dogs are cherished companions in the market scene. Be

aware of and respectful of these furry residents.
- → Tune into the Local Melodies: Local musicians frequently accompany the markets, providing a melodic background to your exploration.
- → Cultural Collage: Look out for stalls that showcase products from different cultures, allowing you to discover the world's treasures in one place.
- → In this market, you're not just a shopper; you're an adventurer, a storyteller, and a participant in a global symphony of cultures.
- → Busing like a local: Utilising the Compass card

As a tourist, imagine that when you board a bus in Brisbane, you're stepping onto more than just a mode of transportation; you're stepping onto a vessel of stories, a time machine that carries the echoes of countless journeys, both mundane and extraordinary.

As you find your seat (get a window seat or a back seat), you're not alone—rather, you're sharing the space with the moments of past commuters who've laughed, cried, and contemplated within these very walls of the bus you are on.

With every ding of the bell, you're joining a chorus of diverse narratives carved from these moments. The park where lovers met, the coffee shop where friendships were born, the office where dreams were pursued—every stop is a nod to the experiences that have unfolded along these routes. The cityscape outside your window seat becomes a moving tapestry, intertwining the lives of Brisbanites across time and space.

Choosing Local Over Convenience

For the thrifty traveller and the curious soul, there's an adventure waiting on the buses of Brisbane. Instead of opting for ride-shares or taxis, endeavour to bus and discover the city from a truly local perspective. These buses are more than just transportation; they're threads that connect you to the heartbeat of the city. Let their routes be your guide, and let the stories within their walls be your companions.

Tips for Navigating Brisbane's Buses:

Recharge Your Compass Card: Instead of relying on ride shares, recharge your Compass card with at least $50. This will ensure smooth travels throughout your stay.

- → Set Up Auto Top-Up: To avoid running low on credit during your stay, set up auto top-up for your Compass card duration. This ensures you're always ready to hop on a bus.
- → Hail Buses and Bus Drivers: Bus drivers do not stop at every stop, like in some places. Make sure to hail the bus to signal to the driver that you intend to board.
- → Use Google Maps for Schedules: For accurate bus schedules and routes, rely on Google Maps instead of the Translink app, which may not always provide reliable information.
- → Avoid Bringing Food: Respect local etiquette by refraining from bringing food on the bus. You'll avoid any issues when boarding.

Remember, as you journey through Brisbane on its buses, you're not just getting from point A to B—you're connecting with the city's heartbeat, touching the essence of its stories, and becoming a part of its ongoing narrative. So, settle into your seat and embrace the time-travelling voyage that these buses offer. As you travel the routes that have been woven into the fabric of Brisbane's existence, you're not just observing; you're participating in the vibrant life that courses through this urban landscape.

Photo by Michael on Unsplash

Footsteps and Echoes of Time: Take a walk in Brisbane City Centre like a local.

The streets of Brisbane are like pages of a well-worn book, each one telling a tale of its own. With every step you take, you're adding your own verse to the chorus of those who've walked these paths before you. Now I am going to make this a little bit dramatic and cinematic.

Walking in the Tracks of History: A Path of Discovery

Picture this: you start your day at the bustling Myer Centre right next to McDonald's in the heart of modern Brisbane. As you step onto the streets, you're embarking on a journey that bridges the past and the present. Your walk takes you across the Brisbane River via the Victoria Bridge, and as you traverse its expanse, imagine the stories of those who've crossed before you—a symphony of footsteps, laughter, and conversations have echoed through time on the Victoria Bridge since 1969. Now pause on the bridge, take in the view, take some selfies and pictures, and continue your walk.

Exploring the Brisbane Museum: Unveiling the Treasures of the Past

Your path leads you to the Brisbane Museum, a treasure trove of history and culture. As you step inside, you're greeted by exhibits that transport you through the ages. From indigenous artefacts that tell the stories of the First Nations people to displays showcasing the city's evolution, you're not just observing relics—you're immersed in a living tapestry that connects you to the heart of Brisbane's past.

Image by qagoma

Journey to the Brisbane Library: Where Stories Take Flight

As your exploration continues, exit on the other side of the museum and make your way to the Brisbane Library, the home of the Brisbane Writer's Festival. This is more than just a repository of books; it's a sanctuary of knowledge and imagination. As you peruse the shelves, you're surrounded by the wisdom of authors and thinkers who've left their mark on the world. Here, your own footsteps become a bridge between the written words and the stories yet to be told.

So I intentionally made this section dramatic so that your journey through Brisbane will become more than a checklist of destinations.

Spiritual Oasis Amidst Urban Splendour: Exploring Historical Places of Worship in Brisbane

Brisbane's diverse landscape isn't only defined by its architectural marvels and urban splendour—it's also enriched by a tapestry of places of worship that reflect the city's cultural richness and history. Beyond their architectural beauty, these centres hold stories, traditions, and faith that resonate with the lives of those who gather within. As you visit these sacred spaces, you'll gain insight into Brisbane's spiritual fabric, discovering that these places of worship are more than just structures; they are gateways to understanding the city's multifaceted identity.

St. John's Cathedral: A Testament to Time

St. John's Cathedral, an Anglican place of worship, stands as an enduring symbol of Brisbane's heritage. Conceived in the late 19th century, its foundation stone was laid in 1901. The cathedral's Neo-Gothic architecture evokes a sense of timelessness and grandeur, while its intricate stained glass windows and richly adorned interiors tell stories of faith and dedication. This historic landmark has witnessed the growth and evolution of Brisbane, serving as a spiritual oasis amidst the city's bustling heart.

Brisbane Synagogue: A Beacon of Faith

The Brisbane Synagogue, established in 1886, holds a special place in the city's history as the oldest synagogue in Queensland. Its graceful Victorian architecture stands as a testament to Brisbane's Jewish community and their enduring faith. As you step inside, you'll find yourself surrounded by tradition, culture, and a sense of continuity that bridges the past with the present.

St. Stephen's Cathedral: An Icon of Catholicism

St. Stephen's Cathedral, located in the heart of the city, is a renowned symbol of Brisbane's Catholic community. Its foundations trace back to the mid-19th century, and the cathedral's design blends Gothic and Romanesque influences. The cathedral's significance transcends its architectural beauty—it serves as a place of worship, reflection, and community for generations of Brisbane residents.

Chung Tian Temple: A Haven of Tranquility

Chung Tian Temple, nestled within the lush surroundings of Priestdale, offers a glimpse into Brisbane's multicultural landscape. This Buddhist temple, built in 1992, embodies the teachings of compassion and harmony. Its traditional Chinese architecture and serene gardens create a haven of tranquillity, inviting visitors to explore the spiritual dimensions of Brisbane's diversity.

Hillsong Church Mount Gravatt: A Modern Note in Brisbane's Spiritual Symphony

For those seeking a modern touch to their spiritual journey, Hillsong Church Mount Gravatt stands as a contemporary beacon within Brisbane's diverse tapestry of worship. The Hillsong Church Brisbane campus reflects a fusion of tradition and innovation. The contemporary architecture mirrors the city's modern skyline, creating a space where worshippers can engage with their faith in a dynamic and inclusive atmosphere.

Visitors to Hillsong Church Mount Gravatt are welcomed into an environment where technology, music, and spirituality converge. The church's commitment to embracing the contemporary while maintaining a focus on faith provides a distinctive addition to Brisbane's spiritual landscape. For those seeking a worship experience that seamlessly integrates tradition with a modern touch, Hillsong Church Mount Gravatt offers a vibrant and relevant option within the spiritual tapestry of Brisbane.

Climate and Seasons

Brisbane enjoys a subtropical climate, which means mild winters and warm summers. In the heart of the Southern Hemisphere, Brisbane unfolds its own symphony of climate and seasons, a melody that dances between the realms of subtropical bliss. Picture the city as a canvas painted with hues of warmth, where nature orchestrates a performance that unfolds in gentle waves of climate.

Wardrobe Cadence: Sunscreen, Hats, and Light Jackets

Consider sunscreen and a hat your trusted companions in this outdoor orchestration. These instruments shield you from the sun's ardent performance, allowing you to dance freely under the celestial spotlight. Picture yourself adorned in a hat, casting a shadow that becomes part of the choreography of your Brisbane experience.

And when the sun takes its bow, a light jacket becomes your accompaniment for the cooler notes that grace the evening air. This versatile layer wraps you in the warmth of comfort, ensuring your journey through Brisbane's nightscape remains as enchanting as the daytime serenade.

Photo by ROMAIN TERPREAU on Unsplash

Pleasant Weather, Outdoor Overture

Brisbane's true brilliance emerges as a testament to its pleasant weather, an overture that beckons you to step outside and join the al fresco celebration. Envision the city as a vibrant stage where outdoor activities unfold like a kaleidoscope of experiences. Whether it's meandering through botanical gardens, strolling along the riverbanks, or partaking in cultural festivals, Brisbane invites you to dance to the rhythm of its climate, a harmonious melody that serenades every moment of your visit.

Chapter 2: Exploring Brisbane's Hidden Gems

Brisbane is a city of diverse neighbourhoods, each offering a unique experience. In this chapter, I'll take you on a journey through some of the most popular areas, sharing my personal favourite spots along the way. I will also introduce some of my favourite lesser-known treasures that make Brisbane a special place.

South Bank: A Cultural Tapestry Unveiled

Embark on your Brisbane adventure at South Bank, a magnetic cultural precinct that weaves together the threads of leisure, art, and natural beauty along the graceful curves of the Brisbane River. Here, where the city's heart meets the water's edge, South Bank beckons with a palette of experiences that will paint your visit with vibrant hues.

South Bank Parklands: Nature's Oasis in the Urban Canvas

Step into the South Bank Parklands, an emerald oasis amid the urban tapestry. This sprawling green haven invites you to lay down a blanket for a picnic, where the whispers of the river mingle with the laughter of picnickers. Immerse yourself in the foliage, where the scent of blossoms accompanies your leisurely strolls along the riverbanks. Picture a mosaic of colours as locals and visitors bask in this enchanting park's subtropical embrace.

Picture by visit.brisbane.com

Wheel of Brisbane: A Spiralling Panorama Above the River's Serenade

Elevate your senses with the Wheel of Brisbane, an iconic structure that spirals gracefully into the skyline. Imagine yourself ascending to new heights, where the cityscape unfolds beneath you like a captivating story. As you peer from your vantage point, the river's serenade becomes a soothing melody, and the urban landscape transforms into a panorama of discovery—a visual symphony that lingers in your memory.

Queensland Art Gallery and Gallery of Modern Art (QAGOMA): A Canvas of Artistic Brilliance

For those attuned to the language of art, the Queensland Art Gallery and Gallery of Modern Art (QAGOMA) stand as pillars of creative brilliance.

Wander through halls adorned with masterpieces, where every stroke and colour tells a story. Imagine sculptures that breathe life into the spaces and exhibits that invite you to traverse the realms of imagination. This is a rendezvous with artistry—an experience that transcends the ordinary and paints your journey with strokes of inspiration.

Photo by Alice Duffield on Unsplash

My favourites: Additional South Bank Gems

Newsflash, none of the above-mentioned perks are my favourite things about Southbank. Read on to discover my favourite things about Southbank. Picture yourself meandering along the Arbour, a boulevard adorned with vibrant magenta bougainvillaea that forms a living tunnel—a botanical embrace that guides your way. Dive into the Streets Beach, a man-made lagoon where the city's rhythm meets the cool waters, providing a unique urban beach experience.

As you explore South Bank, consider venturing into the South Bank Piazza, a cultural hub hosting live performances, markets, and events that add a dynamic rhythm to the precinct. The Cultural Forecourt, with its open-air venues, becomes a stage for festivals, concerts, and celebrations, ensuring there's always a lively crescendo in this cultural tapestry.

Fortitude Valley (the Valley): Where the Night Comes Alive

Dive into the pulsating heart of Brisbane's nightlife by venturing into Fortitude Valley, a neighbourhood that transforms into a kaleidoscope of vibrant energy after the sun sets. Fortitude Valley, also known as "the valley" by locals, invites you to join a nocturnal symphony that echoes with the beats of music, laughter, and the rhythm of the city's after-dark spirit.

Picture from mustdobrisbane.com

Nightlife Extravaganza: Bars, Clubs, and Live Music Venues

As the evening unfolds, Fortitude Valley unveils its dynamic nightlife scene—a playground for those seeking an immersive experience. Imagine a labyrinth of alleys adorned with neon lights, each leading to a different nocturnal adventure. From trendy cocktail bars to pulsating nightclubs, Fortitude Valley caters to every taste. Picture yourself in the midst of live music venues where the air vibrates with the tunes of local and international artists, creating an atmosphere where the night itself becomes a canvas for vibrant expression.

Daytime Exploration: James Street Precinct

James Street during the day is my favourite allure of Fortitude Valley. When the sun graces the sky once again, Fortitude Valley reveals another facet of its charm. Picture yourself strolling through the James Street precinct—a trendy realm where boutique shopping and chic cafes converge. The boutiques beckon with their curated collections, offering a delightful blend of fashion, art, and lifestyle. Take a leisurely pause at one of the sidewalk cafes, where the aroma of freshly brewed coffee mingles with the buzz of the city awakening.

Picture from mustdobrisbane.com

Valley Vignettes: Exploring the Eclectic

Fortitude Valley is not merely a destination for nightlife enthusiasts; it's a canvas that paints eclectic vignettes for every visitor. Imagine street art that adorns the walls, telling stories of creativity and urban expression. Picture yourself amid the eclectic crowd, a mosaic of personalities converging in this neighbourhood where individuality is celebrated.

Brisbane's Chinatown: A Culinary Odyssey

If you are an Asian food fanatic like me, walking from the valley to Chinatown is a must. It is just a stone's throw away from the vibrant energy of Fortitude Valley—an enchanting enclave that adds a touch of the Far East to the city's tapestry. Walk along the lantern-lined streets, where the aroma of authentic Asian cuisine drifts through the air. Picture yourself exploring a myriad of restaurants, serving up delectable dishes that range from traditional dim sum to modern fusion creations.

Picture by sunrisetoday.wordpress.com

New Farm: A Tranquil Haven of Greenery and Gastronomy

When I lived in Brisbane, I travelled to New Farm occasionally, and I always loved it. The area is nestled in the embrace of leafy streets, exuding a trendy charm. New Farm stands as a cherished gem, a place where locals find solace amidst nature's beauty and indulge in culinary delights that define the essence of this vibrant neighbourhood.

Morning Bliss: Jan Powers Farmers Market

Awaken your senses in New Farm with a morning visit to the Jan Powers Farmers Market—a bustling spectacle of freshness and artisanal craftsmanship. Picture yourself strolling through stalls adorned with vibrant produce, the air rich with the scent of herbs and blooming flowers. Engage with local farmers and artisans, their stories becoming part of the tapestry that weaves New Farm's community together. This market isn't just a shopping destination; it's a vibrant social gathering where the pulse of the neighbourhood beats in harmony with the rhythm of the market. I am tempted to suggest my favourite stall at this market, but I will refrain from that. Make sure to explore to the fullest yourself, and I believe you will discover it yourself. Don't hesitate to send me an email if you do discover a favourite stall.

Riverside Serenity: New Farm Park

As the day unfolds, let the tranquillity of New Farm Park draw you in. Imagine a leisurely stroll along the riverfront, where the verdant expanse of New Farm Park becomes a canvas of serenity. Under the shade of giant fig trees, picture yourself finding the perfect spot to unwind. The rustle of leaves, the gentle breeze off the river, and the distant hum of the city—it's a symphony of calmness. The park is a heritage-listed riverfront public park that is adorned with lush greenery and dotted with picnickers.

Culinary Odyssey: Trendy Eateries

New Farm is a culinary odyssey waiting to be explored. Imagine venturing into trendy eateries that line the streets, their menus curated with care and creativity. From cosy cafes to chic restaurants, each venue adds its own flavour to the gastronomic tapestry of New Farm. Picture yourself savouring artisanal dishes, surrounded by an ambience that seamlessly fuses modern sophistication with the neighbourhood's laid-back charm.

Indooroopilly Island Conservation Park: A Tranquil Retreat in Nature's Embrace

Indooroopilly Island Conservation Park is a hidden gem in Brisbane. The place is tucked away from the urban hustle and nestled in a serene embrace of nature. Indooroopilly Island Conservation Park beckons seekers of tranquillity to escape into a peaceful haven. I've been there twice, and each time I go, the city's rhythm disappears in favour of the tranquil sounds of the birds and the gentle whisper of the leaves.

Nature's Canvas: Picnics and Peaceful Repose

If you are a picnic person like me, this should be a good place to start. Imagine stepping into a realm where the vibrant greenery becomes a canvas for relaxation and rejuvenation. Indooroopilly Island Conservation Park offers an idyllic setting for picnics, where the sounds of rustling leaves provide the backdrop for moments of peaceful repose. Picture yourself spreading a blanket under the shade of trees, the sunlight filtering through the foliage, creating a dappled play of light and shadow. This is a sanctuary for those seeking solace in the lap of nature.

Tranquil Trails: Nature Walks Unveiling Hidden Wonders

Embark on nature walks that lead you through winding trails, where every step unveils hidden wonders. Picture yourself meandering along paths embraced by greenery. As you traverse these trails, the symphony of nature becomes your guide, with the soothing sounds of rustling leaves and birdcalls creating a harmonious soundtrack to your journey.

Retreat and Reconnect: A Sanctuary for the Soul
Indooroopilly Island Conservation Park isn't merely a natural escape; it's a sanctuary for the soul, where the urban clamour is replaced by the peaceful symphony of nature. Picture yourself finding a quiet nook, perhaps beside the babbling creek or under the shade of towering trees, where you can retreat and reconnect with the essence of the natural world.

I see Indooroopilly Island Conservation Park as a hidden oasis because, to me, it is a testament to the restorative power of nature, inviting you to escape, unwind, and immerse yourself in the gentle embrace of a pristine natural sanctuary.

Explore the Brisbane River: A CityCat Symphony

Believe it or not, I consider the Brisbane CityCat to be a gem that locals frequently overlook. Embark on a mesmerising journey through the heart of Brisbane by hopping aboard a CityCat ferry—a floating vantage point that transforms the Brisbane River into a liquid highway of discovery. Picture yourself immersed in a symphony of sights, sounds, and stories as you traverse the gentle currents, unveiling unique perspectives of the city's iconic landmarks.

CityCat Elegance: Navigating Brisbane's Liquid Highway

As you step onto the sleek CityCat ferry, envision the vessel gliding across the Brisbane River with an elegance that mirrors the city's own grace. The ferry becomes more than a mode of transportation; it's a floating stage where the river takes centre stage, and the skyline becomes a panoramic backdrop to your aquatic adventure.

Scenic Canvas: Landmarks Unveiled in Splendour

Settle into your seat and let the Brisbane River become your guide, offering panoramic views that unfold like a scenic canvas. Imagine the city's landmarks revealing themselves in splendour—the Story Bridge standing proud, the Kangaroo Point Cliffs looming tall, and the Brisbane Skyline evolving with each passing bend of the river. Every turn presents a new frame for your visual exploration, capturing the essence of Brisbane's architectural diversity.

Photo by Brisbane Local Marketing on Unsplash

BRISBANE UNVEILED

Photo by Valeria Davgon on Unsplash

University of Queensland: Academic Oasis and Blooms of Spring

Part of my 5-year stay in Brisbane was spent at the University of Queensland as a Graduate student. So I believe a visit to Brisbane would be incomplete without exploring the iconic University of Queensland (UQ) campus. Wander through the academic oasis, where knowledge and innovation thrive amidst picturesque surroundings. Don't miss the architectural marvel, the Eleanor Schonell Bridge, offering stunning views of the campus and the Brisbane River.

For a truly enchanting experience, time your visit with spring, when UQ's campuses burst into a kaleidoscope of colour. The annual blooming of the Jacaranda trees paints the landscape in shades of purple, creating a mesmerising sight that's a true testament to the beauty of nature and academia intertwined. Whether you're an academic enthusiast or simply a lover of scenic beauty, the University of Queensland offers a captivating blend of intellect and aesthetics that makes it a must-visit destination in Brisbane.

Picture by UQ

When you visit on any other day, take time to soak in the academic atmosphere, where the pursuit of knowledge is complemented by the allure of nature. Whether you're navigating the impressive architecture of the Great Court or enjoying a peaceful moment by the lakeside, the UQ campus offers an immersive experience that transcends traditional notions of academia.

Chapter 3: Savouring the Culinary Scene and Embracing Nature

Brisbane's culinary scene is a delectable blend of cosmopolitan cuisines and fresh local ingredients. Additionally, Brisbane is surrounded by natural beauty and offers a variety of outdoor activities. In this chapter, I'll walk you through some of my favourite eateries and provide my top tips for embracing nature and adventure.

Picture by thegreatdayout.com.au

Eat Street Northshore: A Culinary Carnival Under the Stars

Step into a realm of gastronomic delight at Eat Street Northshore—a vibrant night market that transcends the ordinary and transforms dining into a culinary carnival. Picture yourself navigating through a maze of food stalls, each offering a treasure trove of flavours that range from exotic Asian street food to decadent gourmet desserts. Here, under the stars, indulge in a unique dining experience that marries diverse cuisines with a lively atmosphere and live entertainment. Caution: Eat Street requires admission fees

Foodie Wonderland: A Treasure Trove of Culinary Delights

As you enter Eat Street Northshore, envision a kaleidoscope of aromas wafting through the air—enticing you to embark on a culinary adventure like no other. Wander through a bustling landscape where food stalls stand like vibrant storefronts, each a portal to a different world of flavours. From sizzling stir-fries to mouthwatering desserts, every stall is a gastronomic gem waiting to be discovered.

Asian Street Food Extravaganza: Flavours from Every Corner

Again, if you are an Asian food fanatic like me, this is the place to be. Imagine yourself immersed in an Asian street food extravaganza, where the sizzle of works and the fragrance of spices create a symphony of culinary delight. Explore stalls that offer dishes from various corners of Asia—spicy noodles, succulent dumplings, and savoury skewers. Imagine yourself navigating this gastronomic journey, sampling flavours that transport you to the bustling street markets of far-off lands.

Gourmet Dessert Oasis: Sweet Temptations

For those with a sweet tooth, envision a gourmet dessert oasis where confections become edible masterpieces. From artisanal chocolates to elaborately crafted pastries, indulge in a symphony of sweet temptations that tantalise your taste buds. Picture yourself savouring each decadent bite under the canopy of twinkling lights, creating a dessert experience that is both visually enchanting and palate-pleasing.

Lively Atmosphere

As the night unfolds, feel the energy of Eat Street Northshore come alive. Envision live entertainment captivating the audience, whether it's soulful tunes, energetic performances, or ambient music that complements the lively atmosphere. The market becomes more than a dining destination; it's a feast for the senses—a place where the vibrancy of food, music, and laughter converges into a symphony of celebration.

Image by Brisbanekids.com.au

Mt. Coot-tha: A Summit Serenade of Panoramic Splendour

Elevate your Brisbane experience by venturing to the majestic heights of Mt. Coot-tha, a natural masterpiece that offers panoramic views of the city and its sprawling surroundings. Whether you embark on a scenic hike or opt for a drive to the lookout, envision a journey that culminates in awe-inspiring vistas, complemented by the tranquil escape of the Brisbane Botanic Gardens nestled at the mountain's base.

Hiking Elevation: A Nature-Infused Ascent

Picture yourself embarking on a nature-infused ascent as you hike up Mt. Coot-tha. The trail unfolds like a story, where each step leads you higher, and the cityscape gradually unveils itself. Envision the crisp mountain air and the rustle of leaves accompanying your journey—a sensory symphony that guides you through lush foliage and native flora. What is the reward for your effort? A summit serenade of panoramic splendour, where the city and its surroundings stretch out before you like a captivating canvas.

Scenic Drive: Effortless Elevation to Magnificent Views

If hiking isn't your preference, imagine a leisurely drive to the summit, where each twist and turn of the road brings you closer to breathtaking views. Picture yourself seated comfortably in a vehicle, the anticipation building with every metre gained in elevation. As you reach the lookout, the city's panorama unfolds beneath you—a breathtaking tapestry of urban and natural beauty that stretches as far as the eye can see.

Image by Brisbanekids.com.au

Brisbane Botanic Gardens: Tranquility at the Mountain's Feet

At the base of Mt. Coot-tha lies the Brisbane Botanic Gardens—a serene oasis that beckons with the promise of tranquillity. Envision yourself strolling through lush pathways, surrounded by a diverse collection of flora from around the world. The Gardens become a haven for leisurely exploration, where vibrant blooms, themed gardens, and the soothing sounds of nature create an atmosphere of serenity.

Image by Must Do Brisbane

Leisurely Stroll: Botanical Bliss in Every Step

Picture a leisurely stroll through the Brisbane Botanic Gardens, where every step reveals a new botanical marvel. The fragrance of blossoms accompanies your journey, and the well-manicured landscapes provide the perfect backdrop for relaxation. As you explore themed gardens and meandering pathways, the gardens become more than just a scenic escape—they are a sanctuary for contemplation and appreciation of the natural world.

Photo by Brisbane Marketing

Moreton Island: An Aquatic Wonderland of Adventure and Serenity

Take a ferry to Moreton Island for a day of snorkelling and sandboarding. Crystal-clear waters host vibrant marine life, offering a snorkelling extravaganza. Climb the island's dunes for an adrenaline-pumping sandboarding thrill. As the sun sets, participate in the enchanting ritual of dolphin feeding. Balmy beaches provide tranquil retreats, creating an island odyssey of relaxation and adventure—a paradise just a ferry ride away from Brisbane.

Picture by brisbane.qld.gov.au

Ferry Ride: A Seafaring Prelude to Paradise

Envision the anticipation building as you board the ferry from Brisbane, bound for the azure shores of Moreton Island. The sea breeze becomes your companion as the vessel glides across the water, setting the stage for the tropical adventure that awaits. Picture yourself on the deck, watching the city skyline fade into the distance, making way for the untouched beauty of Moreton Island.

Snorkelling Extravaganza: Underwater Marvels Unveiled

As you arrive on Moreton Island, picture yourself donning snorkelling gear and immersing yourself in an underwater realm of vivid colours and marine life. The crystal-clear waters become a canvas of coral gardens, where tropical fish dance in a symphony of hues. Imagine yourself snorkelling amidst the vibrant marine tapestry, discovering the intricate beauty of the island's underwater wonders.

Picture by moretonislandadventures

Sandboarding Thrills: Dunes of Endless Adventure

Feel the rush of adrenaline as you climb the sandy peaks of Moreton Island's dunes. Picture the panoramic views from the summit and the island's coastline stretching before you. Now, envision the exhilaration as you descend on a sandboard, carving your way down the dunes—a thrilling experience that blends adventure with the natural beauty of this island oasis.

Dolphin Feeding: Sunset Serenade with Marine Companions

As the day gracefully progresses, imagine the enchanting opportunity to feed dolphins at sunset. Picture yourself on the shore, the sun casting a warm glow over the water as friendly dolphins approach. Engage in this magical moment, where human and marine life converge in a serenade of connection, creating memories that transcend the ordinary.

Relaxation Haven: Balmy Beaches and Tranquil Retreats

Beyond the adventure, envisage moments of relaxation on Moreton Island's balmy beaches. Picture yourself lounging in the sun or strolling along the shoreline, the rhythmic sounds of waves providing a backdrop to your island retreat. Moreton Island offers pockets of tranquillity where you can unwind, reflect, and appreciate the untouched beauty of this coastal haven.

Picture by @drew_j_brown on queensland.com

Bribie Island: Coastal Serenity Unveiled

Moreton Bay snorkelling requires a little bit of travelling, and so does Bribie Island. But trust me, they are worth teh travel. Journey just a short drive from Brisbane to the tranquil shores of Bribie Island. Cross the bridge, leaving the mainland behind and entering a realm where coastal bliss awaits.

Sun-Drenched Haven

Step onto the island's shores and witness the expansive coastline—a sun-drenched haven inviting leisurely strolls, sun-soaked afternoons, and communion with the gentle rhythm of the waves.

Exploring Nature's Sanctuary

Immerse yourself in Bribie Island National Park, where lush landscapes, diverse birdlife, and secluded trails create a sanctuary for nature enthusiasts. Traverse this preserved paradise, surrounded by the sounds of coastal flora and fauna.

Aquatic Exploration

For aquatic adventurers, visualize gliding across the calm waters of the Pumicestone Passage. Kayak or paddleboard with the Glass House Mountains providing a majestic backdrop to your aquatic exploration.

Breathtaking Sunset Spectacle

As the day transitions into the evening, picture a breathtaking sunset over the Pumicestone Passage, casting a warm glow across the horizon. Bribie Island becomes an aquatic wonderland inviting you to explore, rejuvenate, and savour coastal serenity.

Photo By Redland City Council | Licensed Under Cc By-Nd 2.0

Stradbroke Island: Coastal Paradise Unveiled

Talking of a long journey, Stradbroke Island is another discovery I made through long road travels from Brisbane that was definitely worth the journey. It is a popular place known to the locals as Stradie.

Embark on a journey just off the coast of Brisbane to the pristine shores of North Stradbroke Island—an idyllic retreat where natural beauty and coastal charm seamlessly converge.

Island Gateway: Crossing the Waters

Imagine the anticipation as you board the ferry, leaving behind the mainland and setting sail for the azure waters surrounding Stradbroke Island. The short voyage becomes a prelude to the coastal paradise awaiting your arrival.

Sandy Shores and Turquoise Waters: Island Bliss

Step onto Stradbroke's shores, where white sandy beaches stretch along the coastline, inviting you to bask in the sun, take leisurely walks, or immerse yourself in the refreshing waters of the Pacific Ocean. The island's natural beauty becomes a canvas for relaxation and exploration.

Exploring the Diverse Landscapes: Nature's Tapestry

Visualize the diverse landscapes of Stradbroke Island, from the lush flora of the interior to the rugged beauty of the coastline. Wander through the Gorge Walk and witness breathtaking views of the ocean, or explore the island's rich cultural history at Dunwich and Amity Point.

Marine Adventures: Aquatic Wonderland

For those seeking aquatic adventures, picture yourself diving into the crystal-clear waters for a snorkelling expedition or riding the waves as you try your hand at surfing. Stradbroke Island's surrounding waters offer an aquatic wonderland for enthusiasts of all kinds.

Sunset Serenade: Nature's Farewell

As the day gracefully transitions into the evening, envision a captivating sunset over the horizon—the perfect conclusion to your island escapade. Stradbroke Island becomes more than a destination; it's a coastal paradise inviting you to explore, unwind, and revel in the natural splendour that defines this island sanctuary.

Lone Pine Koala Sanctuary: An Aussie Wildlife Haven

It's not really one of my top-most places but Nestled along the Brisbane River, the Lone Pine Koala Sanctuary stands as a cherished haven for wildlife enthusiasts and those eager to get up close with Australia's iconic creatures. Imagine entering a realm where the charm of native fauna takes centre stage.

Visualise strolling through eucalyptus-scented pathways, encountering kangaroos lounging under the sun, and witnessing the playful antics of wallabies. Lone Pine offers an interactive experience, allowing you to hand-feed these marsupials and forge unforgettable connections.

The highlight? Imagine holding a koala in your arms, capturing a moment frozen in time—a quintessential Australian encounter. Learn about the sanctuary's conservation efforts and engage with the passionate caretakers who share their knowledge about the unique wildlife residing within these natural confines.

As you traverse the sanctuary, from the vast open spaces to the diverse aviaries, picture immersing yourself in the rich biodiversity of Australia. Lone Pine Koala Sanctuary isn't merely a visit; it's an invitation to witness the beauty of native fauna, contribute to conservation, and create lasting memories surrounded by the enchanting wildlife of the Land Down Under.

Image by Prostooleh on Freepik

Chapter 4: Mastering the Art of Local-ism

If you read this guide until this chapter, you should get the vibe that I am nearing the end of my recommendations. In this chapter, I will go through a few must-learns I had to embrace in order to bond with the locals. To become a true Brisbanite, you've got to do as the locals do.

Here's your guide to infiltrating the ranks:

Embrace the Outdoors: Brisbane's Active Lifestyle

Immerse yourself in Brisbane's vibrant outdoor culture. Picture joining in a morning jog along the river, where the sun paints the sky with warm hues. Imagine cycling through the city's dedicated bike lanes, the urban landscape unfolding before you. Alternatively, find solace in a park, surrounded by nature, with a good book in hand. Brisbane's active lifestyle invites you to embrace the outdoors—whether it's the invigorating pulse of a morning run, the freedom of cycling through the cityscape, or the simple joy of unwinding in a green oasis. Seriously, though, make sure to try cycling. It's beautiful and scenic.

Café Culture: Sip and Savour in Brisbane's Charm

Immerse yourself in Brisbane's bustling café culture. Envision ordering a perfectly crafted flat white or a rich, long black. The aroma tantalises your senses. Picture yourself seated at a local café, the ambience alive with conversation and the clinking of cups. As you sip your coffee, become a part of the vibrant tapestry of Brisbane, where each café embodies the city's charm. Whether you're people-watching or simply relishing the moment, Brisbane's café culture invites you to savour the art of coffee and soak in the city's lively atmosphere.

Learn the Lingo: Aussie Slang 101

Immerse yourself in the local vibe by mastering Aussie slang.

Greet with a cheerful "G'day," plan to catch up in the "arvo" (afternoon), and start your day with a hearty "brekkie" (breakfast).

Embrace phrases like "mate" for a friend and "no worries" for a laid-back attitude.

Aussie slang isn't just words; it's a cultural handshake. Pick up these colloquial gems, and soon you'll be conversing like a true local, adding a dash of Down Under charm to your Brisbane experience. No worries, mate!

During my time in Brisbane, I found these lingos easy to pick up. So you might want to start with these:

- → G'day: Australian greeting.
- → Mate: Friend or buddy.
- → Arvo: Afternoon.
- → Brekkie: Breakfast.
- → Barbie: Barbecue.
- → Heaps: A lot or many.

- → Maccas: McDonald's.
- → No worries: Don't mention it, or it's okay.
- → Thongs: Flip-flops.
- → Esky: Portable cooler for drinks.
- → Aussie: Australian.
- → Cuppa: A cup of tea or coffee.
- → Footy: Often referring to rugby.
- → Ripper: Excellent or fantastic.

Photo from broncos.com.au

Cheer for the Local Teams: Brisbane's Sporting Spirit

Immerse yourself in Brisbane's sporting fervour by cheering for the local teams. Feel the adrenaline at Suncorp Stadium during thrilling rugby matches, where the crowd's energy becomes infectious, especially when supporting the local rugby team, the Broncos. Dive into the excitement of the Australian Football League (AFL) season, supporting the Brisbane Lions with passion. Whether you're a seasoned sports enthusiast or a casual spectator, embracing the city's teams is a gateway to the heart of Brisbane's communal spirit. Join in the cheers, wear the team colours, and be part of the electric atmosphere that defines Brisbane's love for sports.

Chapter 5: Connect with Events and Festivals

Brisbane pulsates with life through its diverse events and festivals, celebrating its vibrant culture. Dive into the heart of the city's festivities with these immersive experiences.

Brisbane Festival: A September Extravaganza

Dive into a cultural feast at the annual Brisbane Festival, held in September. Immerse yourself in a tapestry of arts, music, and theatre, where the city transforms into a vibrant stage of creativity. Envision attending mesmerising performances that captivate the senses and showcase Brisbane's artistic pulse. As the festival reaches its pinnacle, don't miss the breathtaking Riverfire fireworks display—a dazzling spectacle that lights up the night sky, symbolising the culmination of this month-long celebration. The Brisbane Festival is not just an event; it's a collective celebration of the city's artistic soul, inviting you to join in the revelry and create lasting memories.

The Ekka: August Extravaganza

Mark your calendar for the annual Ekka, a quintessential Brisbane experience held each August. Picture an amalgamation of agriculture, entertainment, and community spirit coming together in a lively showcase. Imagine wandering through bustling exhibition halls where local produce, arts, and crafts take centre stage.

Feel the thrill of carnival rides and games, creating an atmosphere of excitement. From animal shows to live music, The Ekka offers a diverse range of experiences for all ages. As August unfolds, join in the festivities, savouring the unique blend of tradition and modernity that defines this iconic Brisbane event.

Photo by Concrete Playground

Brisbane Asia Pacific Film Festival: Cinematic Celebration

Immerse yourself in the magic of cinema at the Brisbane Asia Pacific Film Festival. This annual celebration, held in Brisbane, brings together a diverse array of films from the Asia-Pacific region. Envision a cinematic journey through compelling narratives, thought-provoking documentaries, and visually stunning masterpieces. Picture yourself in the midst of filmmakers, enthusiasts, and storytellers, sharing a collective passion for the art of filmmaking. As the festival unfolds, embrace the cultural richness and cinematic brilliance that permeate the city, making this event a must-attend for cinephiles and those seeking a unique window into the cinematic landscapes of the

Asia Pacific.

Photo by Brisbane Festival

Photo by Brisbane Festival

Post Commentary

As you delve into this unconventional travel guide to Brisbane, it's essential to note that every suggestion and recommendation stems from my personal experiences and genuine affection for this vibrant city. None of the recommended places are sponsored; they're chosen based on the joy and memories they brought me during my time in Brisbane.

This guide is a testament to my unique journey, and I encourage every reader to approach it with the same spirit of exploration. Each suggested place is a gem I've uncovered and enjoyed, and I genuinely believe that anyone who follows this guide will discover the charm and allure that Brisbane has to offer.

So, as you embark on your own Brisbane adventure, consider this guide not as a checklist but as an invitation to immerse yourself in the city's soul. Try and visit each suggested place, savour the experiences, and create your own memories. I'm confident you won't regret it, and I hope this guide adds a touch of authenticity to your Brisbane escapade. Safe travels!

About The Author

Allow me to introduce myself. My name is MegdeRoayle (owner of CravedM Creations), and I'm a Ghanaian living in the vibrant city of Brisbane, Australia. From the moment I wake up to the time I rest my head on the pillow, my life is a fascinating blend of devotion, learning, and hard work.

My unwavering faith as a devout Christian with a Pentecostal passion has been my guiding light throughout my journey. It's what keeps me grounded, inspired, and motivated to strive for excellence in everything I do. I've always believed that my purpose extends beyond the boundaries of my own life, and I'm committed to making a positive impact on those around me.

One of my greatest joys is diving into the world of learning. You'll often find me with my nose buried in books, soaking up knowledge across various subjects. Whether it's delving into the depths of theology, exploring the intricacies of human behaviour, or unravelling the mysteries of storytelling, I'm a lifelong student hungry for new insights.

But don't be mistaken; I'm not just a bookworm. I've earned a reputation as a dedicated workaholic, channelling my energy into everything I undertake. Whether it's crafting engaging stories, developing captivating content, or connecting with readers, I approach each task with the same level of enthusiasm and dedication.

My journey from Ghana to Australia has been an incredible one, allowing me to experience the beauty of different cultures, landscapes, and people. The diversity and richness of life have fueled my creativity and broadened my perspectives, shaping the stories I tell and the ideas I share.

Printed in Great Britain
by Amazon